PRO-LIFE KIDS!

written by
BETHANY BOMBERGER

illustrated by
ED KOEHLER

BARA PUBLISHING

ISBN: 978-0-9972036-7-7
Library of Congress Control Number - 2019914411

Printed in the U.S.A
Signature Book Printing
www.sbpbooks.com

Published by Bara Publishing
BaraPublishing.com

For inquiries: *info@barapublishing.com*

Book editing, design and layout by Ryan Scott Bomberger

First printing edition 2019

BARA
PUBLISHING

Dedication

To Ryan – my best friend and the most amazing husband.
You are my rock. Thank you for your endless hours of speaking
LIFE into our family and people around the world.
I adore you. 😍

To my precious children – Radiance, Kai, Aliyah and Justice.
I love you with everything in me. My prayer is that you would
love God with all of your hearts, live for Him and always see
others the way God does. 😘

To my true friends and family who encourage me
with laughter, hugs and prayers that fuel God dreams. 🔥

Pro-life means *for life*.
We're **cheering** for you.
Your life is important.
There's only one you.

You're special. Just right.
You're **one of a kind.**
The world needs your talents,
your heart, and your mind.

God made you unique.
You have no clone.
Your **fingerprints** are yours.
Yes, yours alone.

He knit you together
one cell at a time...
with **love** and attention—
a plan so divine.

It doesn't matter
your **size** or your age.
You have **equal** value
whatever the stage.

And where you live won't determine your **worth.**

You're a person. It's true! Even before your birth.

Sadly, there are those who **don't** understand...

that life has **purpose**
whether planned *or* unplanned.

Throughout history many believed a **lie.**

"You're not a person!"
"No way!" they cried.

Today many think
that lie is still true—
that **babies** in wombs
aren't people too.

Abortion is when
some say it's okay
to take that baby's
precious life away.

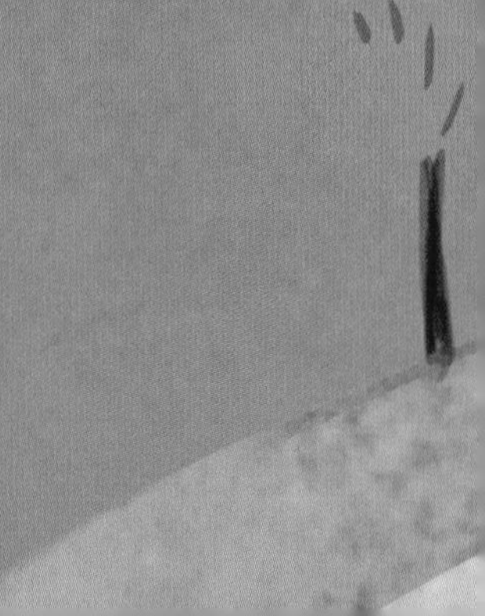

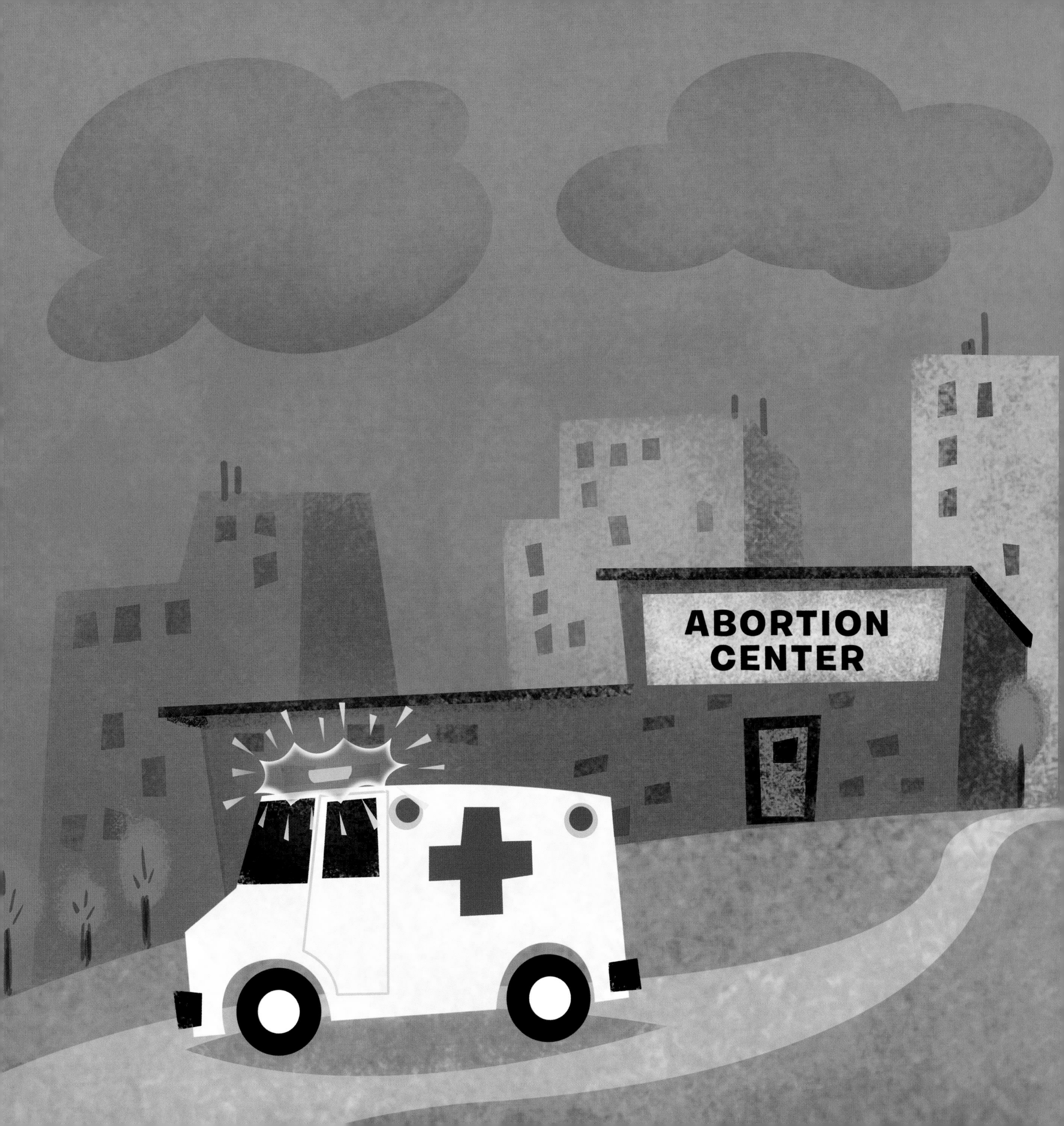
ABORTION
CENTER

But
your color, your gender
and nationality,
your abilities, looks
and **great** personality...

They make you – *you*.
Fully human, indeed.
No exceptions. No exclusions.
That's the Pro-Life creed!

Like many before us
who stood for what's **right,**

we'll *never* give up as we fight for life.

Let it be known
we're glad **you're** alive.

Our world is better
because you've arrived!

So, speak up for life.
Raise your voice.
Speak up for those silenced
who have no choice.

Speak to anyone
who needs to know truth.
Speak about life to every
adult, child and youth.

So abortion **lies**
will all be shattered
as more hearts believe
humanity matters!

One day you will see
that all you have done
was worth every moment
to **save** even one.

'Cause when you reach one,
and I do too—
before we know it,
we'll see **breakthrough!**

The culture of life
will continue to grow.
It'll spread across nations
the more love we show.

Moms and dads
will choose **loving** options.
They'll parent their child
or place for **adoption.**

Someone, somewhere is depending on **you**

to fight for their **worth** and cheer for them too.

Join **millions** of us in cities and towns

EQUAL JUSTICE UNDER LAW

who are pro-life **and will never** back down.

We are Pro-Life Kids
so dreams come **alive.**
We are Pro-Life Kids
so our future **survives.**

We are Pro-Life Kids
'til injustice ends!
We are Pro-Life Kids.
It's life we defend!

We are Pro-Life Kids.
That's **you** and that's **me.**

We impact our world
and change destinies.

Dear Reader,

My name is Bethany Bomberger. I wrote this book with YOU in mind!

I want you to know that you are so special and loved.

My husband, Ryan, and I have spent a lot of time making sure that you know that every life has God-given purpose. Yes, you are valuable, and our world is a better place because you exist!

There are people who do not agree with us and believe that abortion — ending the life of a baby before it is born — is okay. Ryan and I join millions of other pro-life people, like you, who want abortion to end.

It is our dream that every single person — whether planned or unplanned, able or differently-abled — will have a chance to live life to the fullest!

Wherever you are on this great planet, we pray that you would follow your heart and stand up for LIFE.

With Love,

Bethany Bomberger

Proverbs 31:8-9: "Speak up for those who cannot speak for themselves; ensure justice for those being crushed. Yes, speak up for the poor and helpless, and see that they get justice." (NLT)

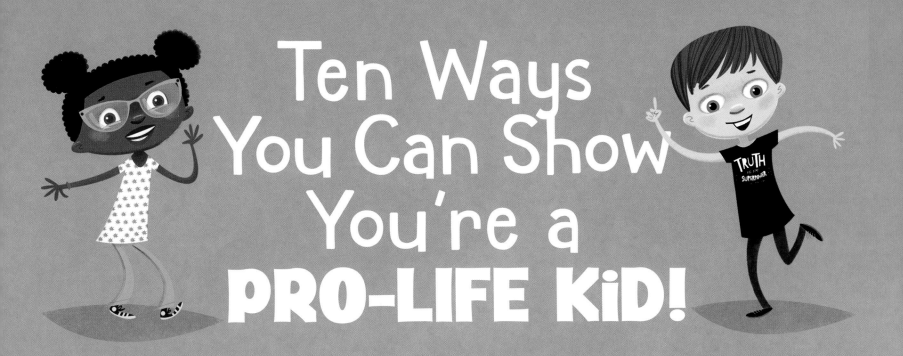

Ten Ways You Can Show You're a PRO-LIFE KiD!

1. Share this book with others.

2. Pray that abortion will end.

3. Always be kind! Set an example and show others that every human life is important.

4. Help collect diapers and baby items for your local pregnancy resource center. (They love to help families in need!)

5. If you were adopted, share your story.

7. Wear a pro-life shirt to show the truth to others.

8. Send a letter to your local/state/federal leaders encouraging them to pass laws to protect moms and their babies.

9. Invite your friends to a pro-life event.

10. Choose to march for LIFE in DC or in your own state.

MEET REAL PRO-LIFE KIDS!

Radiance (Rai Rai) loves visiting local pregnancy resource centers. She knows that when mommies are scared about having a baby, the people working at these centers care for and help them. She prays for these moms and their babies. She enjoys helping to create new and fun pro-life t-shirts, too. Rai Rai believes her generation can end the sadness and violence of abortion.

Mikai loves seeing pro-life friends and meeting new people from around the world at the March for Life in DC. Mikai boldly shares with others that he is pro-life. He believes that babies are valuable even before they are born! He's not shy about speaking up for those who cannot speak for themselves.

Aliyah is a gifted singer. She loves to use her voice to sing for those who haven't had a chance to use theirs. She has sung at many events in front of thousands and reminds people that every life has purpose. And she just loooooooves wearing her pro-life t-shirts and adding her own style!

Justice knows that adoption is an awesome option. He knows this because he is adopted and loved. As a very young boy he spoke to reporters about adoption. He wants to teach others to be brave and defend Life too.

Sophia and her sisters, Lilly and Gracie, love to pray for the end of the violence of abortion. They pray at home and at church. People take notice of their shirts with pro-life messages. Sophia, a middle school student, was a bold prayer leader at the annual OneVoiceDC event in Washington DC!

Stephen, Bethany, Kimberly, David, and Johnny are pro-life kids. They have taken time to learn about what it means to be pro-life when they attended a Pro-Life Kid's Class. They proudly wear their t-shirts that encourage others to stand for everyone's Right to Life.

Xavier, Elize, and Blaize are really creative. They have figured out a number of ways to show the world they are pro-life. Xavier runs a lemonade stand on summer days. Elize sells girls' hair bows. Both siblings donate a portion of the money they make to pro-life causes. Their brother, Blaize, loves to help too! These siblings also join their parents in praying outside of abortion centers. They love to hand out blessing bags to moms who are worried about their pregnancy.

Abigail, Reuben, and Joseph love to boldly wear their pro-life gear around town, to classes and to stores. They've been able to see images of their baby sister, Sarah, way before she was even born. Now that she's arrived, they get to love her and teach her how to be pro-life too.

Eva has eight siblings. Three of her siblings were adopted. Eva and her family know that adoption is so important. Eva courageously wrote a pro-life essay and entered it in a library writing contest. She was so excited when she won second place. Lots of other people were able to read it too!

Joey is a pro-life kid! His mom is a singer and musician so he goes to pro-life events all over the nation with his parents. He wears his pro-life shirts and loves to pray for moms, dads and children. He can't wait to share what it means to be pro-life with his adorable baby sister, Eliana.

The Lott Family is a super special family! They are made up of biological and adopted siblings. They know that every life is special. Mr. and Mrs. Lott started FaithfulAdoptionConsultants.com to help families who want to adopt. The eight Lott children – Mina, Michael, Carson, Aidan, Aniya, Emmy, Collier and Zeke – love babies and want the world to know that every one of them should have a chance at life. They've been featured in a bunch of fun Radiance Foundation videos about adoption and even on a huge billboard!

Ezra and Abdias pray for the end of abortion. They go with their mom to pray outside of a nearby abortion center for other moms who are scared about being pregnant. Their church has a ministry that helps support their local pregnancy care center. They love being pro-life and sharing with their baby sister, Rinnah, how precious every life is before and after being born.

Reagan and Austin are the youngest of five. Although they lived far away from Washington DC for most of their lives, they would dream about marching for life in our nation's capital. In 2019, they moved to the DC area and made the trip with their mom, dad and friends who share the belief that we're all created equal. Austin loved seeing so many different signs. Reagan loved seeing thousands of other kids marching for the same cause.

Heaven, Trinity, Eden, Joseph, Justus and their siblings know that every life is important. They pray that others will learn that all babies are a gift from God. They have been part of a Pro-Life Kids class. They like to share about why they believe every life has purpose and are willing prayer leaders. They are confident that when other kids understand what it means to be pro-life, they will want to help protect mamas and their babies.

Grace's mom used to work inside a Planned Parenthood abortion center. She left when Grace was very little. Although she doesn't remember that day, Grace has grown up knowing that life is sacred. She prays in front of abortion centers, passes out tiny fetal models, and goes to pregnancy center banquets to listen to her mom speak about rescuing moms, babies and even abortion workers. She said: "My parents raised me to be a pro-life kid. I'm really thankful that they have. I can't even imagine being a person who believes it is ever okay to take the life of a child. I'm proud that my mom is so brave."

PRO-LIFE KiDS! PLEDGE

I pledge to protect and value all human life.
I will be a voice for the unborn.

I AM A PRO-LIFE KID!

PROVERBS 31:8–9

_____
MY NAME

_____
DATE

TAKE A PICTURE WITH YOUR PLEDGE, AND SEND IT TO US AT PROLIFEKIDS.COM!

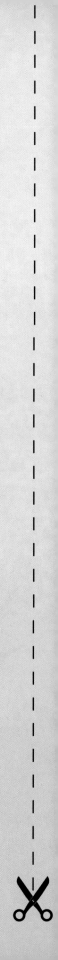

About the Author

Bethany Bomberger has been an educator for two decades. She has taught in both public and private schools, working with thousands of children, youth and adults of all ages. With a Bachelor's Degree in Education and Family Studies and a Master's Degree in Education from Regent University, Bethany has spearheaded innovative educational programs in her classrooms and the communities where she lived. She is the Co-Founder (along with her hubby) and Executive Director of The Radiance Foundation, a life-affirming organization that is rooted in the belief that we are all created in God's image and have undeniable purpose. As a public speaker, she addresses large and diverse audiences with inspiring messages of faith, hope and Christ's love. Married to her best friend, Ryan, Bethany is an adoptive mama who loves to celebrate courageous birthmoms and the beauty of adoption. She embraces the challenge and the blessing of homeschooling her four bold and compassionate pro-life kids: Rai Rai, Kai, Aliyah and Justice. www.Radiance.life

About the Illustrator

Ed Koehler is an amazing freelance illustrator from St. Louis, MO. He specializes in fun, lively art for children's books, educational materials, and a variety of print and online products. Ed's incredible work has been published around the world and has received many awards from the Evangelical Press Association and Associated Church Press. Ed designs and illustrates projects as varied as multi-media stage sets, environmental graphics, and curriculums. He is an artist with incredible talent and enthusiasm! Ed is a member of the Society of Children's Book Writers and Illustrators, and the St. Louis Artists Guild. EdKoehler.com

Learn more at
PROLIFEKiDS.COM